Barcelona and Gaudí.

Examples of Modernist architecture

I dedicate this book to my daughter Florencia Kliczkowski Wladimirski

H. A. K.

Barcelona and Gaudí. Examples of Modernist architecture

Publisher: Paco Asensio

Photographs: © Miquel Tres

Text: Raül Garcia i Aranzueque

Translation: Harry Paul

Coordination: Susana González

Art director: Mireia Casanovas Soley

Layout: Emma Termes Parera, Soti Mas-Bagà

Photographs pp. 68 to 71:
© Pere Planells: 16, 20, 23, 25, 27, 29, 30
© Melba Levick: 17, 18, 19, 21, 22, 24, 26, 28, 48

Copyright for the international edition:
© Kliczkowski Publisher-A Asppan S.L.
Fundición, 15. Polígono Industrial Sta. Ana
28529 Rivas-Vaciamadrid. Madrid
Tel.: +34 91 666 50 01
Fax: +34 91 301 26 83
asppan@asppan.com
www.onlybook.com

ISBN: 84-89439-65-6
D.L.: B-38.680-01

Editorial project:

LOFT Publications
Domènec, 9 2-2
08012 Barcelona. Spain
Tel.: +34 93 218 30 99
Fax: +34 93 237 00 60
e-mail: loft@loftpublications.com
www.loftpublications.com

Printing:
Anmann Artes Gráficas. Sabadell. Barcelona

October 2001

Examples of Modernist architecture

3

1. Plaça Reial lampposts

2. Hotel España

3. Hotel Peninsular

4. Casa Figueras

5. Acadèmia de Ciències i Arts

6. Editorial Montaner i Simón

7. Casa Fargas

8. Lamppost-benches by P. Falqués

9. Conservatori M. de Música

10. Casa Thomas

11. Can Serra

12. Casa Comalat

13. Palau del Baró de Quadras

14. Casa Macaya

15. Museu de Zoologia

Continuation

Practical information and Routes

The façade of the Palau del Baró de Quadras, today the Museu de la Música

Modernism bequeathed Catalunya, and Barcelona in particular, with a good number of architectural works of art. Some of them are true masterpieces famous across the world, among these being constructions like the Sagrada Família Temple and Parc Güell by the Modernist architect par excellence Antoni Gaudí. These designs have become more than just architectural or aesthetic landmarks; they are icons and symbols which represent the Catalan capital. Crowds of tourists from all over the world flock to these sites, cameras and videos at the ready as they try to capture the inspiring beauty of Gaudí's creations.

However, the main attraction of Modernism for the visitor to Barcelona is not to contemplate a handful of acclaimed buildings —though they shouldn'the fail to do this— but to discover the small wonders which the architects left all

The vestibule of the Casa Thomas

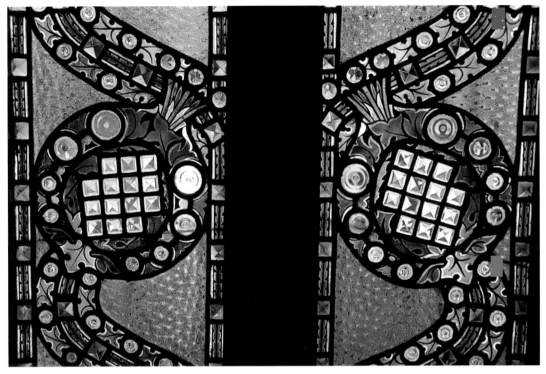

Stained glass windows inside the Casa Thomas

over the city. Modernism is everywhere, especially in the Eixample neighbourhood. It can be found in private Bourgeois houses from the epoch, restaurants, shops and even in street furnishings. This artistic movement—closely associated with art nouveau—found its way into all the ambiences and therefore to understand the extent to which it impacted on society it is necessary to move away from the great symbols and focus in on the little things and places which set the scene for everyday life.

None of the works featured in this book is an icon, nor do they appear on the front pages of any guide book or presentation of the city. However, each house, each shop, or even each lamppost is undoubtedly of artistic value and hides away a small part of history. They all have *Each work is undoubtedl of artistc value and hides away a small part of history* a story worth telling and will help us to get a fuller picture of this artistic movement which had its epicenter in Catalonia, and in the capital, Barcelona.

For many years Barcelona neglected its fabulous Modernist heritage. Architectural jewels like the benches and lampposts blended into one on Passeig de Gràcia, or building facades like the endlessly photographed Casa

The interior patio of the Palau del Baró de Quadras

Milà, known as the Pedrera (Stone Quarry) were allowed to deteriorate and become grimy until eventually they had a sorry look. Fortunately, in the nineteen nineties the City Hall realised this could not go on and undertook positive action to recover the artistic heritage. Campaigns like "Barcelona, posa't guapa" ("Barcelona, bring out your beauty") have radically changed the aspect of most of the old buildings of the urban area.

At the same time the City Hall gave a promotional push to the Modernist Route, a trip around the most represen- tative works of this artistic movement. This tour around the city is well- signposted and mapped out with red, round paving stones on the street surface to guide visitors.

As well as local

Stained glass windows at the Acadèmia de Ciències i Arts

A lamppost in the Plaça Reial

A lamppost-bench designed by Pere Falqués, next to the Pedrera

government, private enterprise also started to sponsor this effort to bring out the best of Barcelona. Many buildings which before were for private use were reclaimed for the people, and visitors, of the city. For example, some private bourgeois homes of the turn of the century were given a new lease of life as museums. This is the case of the old publishing company Montaner i Simón, the headquarters of which since 1984 houses the Fundació Antoni Tàpies. The old Palau del Baró de Quadras is today the city's Museu de la Música. However, while it is true that some Modernist buildings switched over to public uses, there are still a considerable number of privately owned homes not open to visitors. Any inquisitive visitor smitten by curiosity will have to get round the porter or find some other way of getting in. Even if you could not see inside, the façades alone are well worth a look.

Over the years more and more buildings belonging to the Modernist heritage have been converted to public uses

This book is intended to be an aid to any visitor who wants to go deeper than just taking in the traditional tourist sites so that they can discover how a group of artists created a trend which broke away from the old established ideas and changed the city's physiognomy.

Plaça Reial lampposts 1878

Antoni Gaudí 1852-1926

Plaça Reial

Some symbols of Catalanism can be appreciated, such as the flower patterns, mythological animals, and the coat of arms of the city. Gaudí rounded off the design by reworking neo-grecian details with a tendency towards realism.

The plaza Reial is one of the most buzzing places in the city. People from all walks of life and from all over the world stroll beneath its arches everyday, let off energy dancing in the bars at night, or just rest their backpack by the side of the fountain of the Tres Gràcies in the middle.

The cosmopolitan atmosphere of the square has not gone unnoticed by writers and cinema directors who have often drawn on this inspiration to create their stories. However, the down side of the square's fame is that the neighbours sometimes get fed up with the round the clock noise and have hung banners protesting out on their balconies.

This porticoed square, created by the architect and urban design Francesc Daniel Molina in 1848, based on the French style of the Napoleonic epoch, is blessed with having a little touch added by Gaudí. In 1878 the City Hall, as part of a city wide project to place richly varied lampposts in many streets and squares, commissioned the young architect–he had not then even graduated from the Faculty of Architecture–with the task of coming up with two lampposts to flank the fountain.

The lampposts reveal that even at an early age Gaudí was bursting with talent and creativity: they cleverly combine the latest technology of the period (gaslight and afterwards electric light) with a vanguardist design.

The recent restoration of the lampposts did not please some people of the city who considered the red and yellow tones used to be too loud.

The Plaça Reial is a powerful magnet for foreign visitors. On summer nights it is often difficult to find a free table among the numerous open-air bars around the square.

Ħotel España 1903

Lluís Domènech i Montaner 1850-1923

Carrer Sant Pau, 9-11

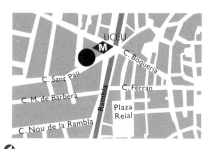

This hotel in the Carrer Sant Pau, very close to the Teatre del Liceu, can boast of having been decorated by three of the leading lights of Catalan Modernism: the architect Lluís Domènech i Montaner, the sculptor Eusebi Arnau and the painter Ramon Casas. In 1903 the decoration of the building was put into the hands of Domènech i Montaner who converted the ground floor walls into a sea of waves teeming with marine fauna like fishes, starfishes and even mermaids. The distinguished painter Ramon Casas was called in to do the wall paintings.

The decorative elements which explain the hotel's name are to be found low down on the wall. Dozens of medallions with the coats of arms of different Spanish cities are engraved into the rather original wooden skirting board, complete with its floral patterns.

Eusebi Arnau left his mark with a magnificent alabaster sculpture ensemble next to the restaurant.

Today the hotel's restaurant is on the ground floor. There is also a pleasant, bright interior patio.

The carved wood frieze with flower patterns and ceramic medallions reveal the importance the Modernist designers attached to the decorative elements.

Ꞡotel Peninsular 1875

Architect unknown

Carrer Sant Pau, 34

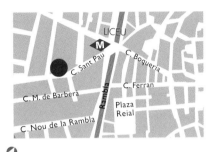

The Hotel Peninsular is another example of the influence of Modernism on the bourgeois class of that time. Businessmen were becoming increasingly willing to invest their money in projects related to the leisure time of the ever-growing well-off classes of Barcelona. Logically, the owners of restaurants and hotels set out to make their establishments attractive to these new classes and Modernism was a lead player in this process of renovating the city.

The most outstanding feature, and one which reveals the Modernist credentials of the hotel is the interior patio. The corridors are long, the doors grand and the ceilings high. The patio is decorated with ceramic tiles arranged in straight lines, illuminated by the light coming down through the skylight also reaching the galleries. The cream painted walls and the abundance of plants on the galleries produces a balanced and stimulating colour composition.

The hotel was restored at the end of the nineteen eighties, regaining a great deal of its Modernist individuality.

Before being a hotel the building was a convent of the Agustine order. If you look closely it is not difficult to image the monks and friars wondering around with books as they go about their monasterial duties. The building was converted into a hotel in 1876 and enjoyed its moment of maximum splendor during the Exposición Universal in Barcelona in 1888.

The squared pattern formed by the ceramic floor tiles bestows a great deal of character on the establishment. The restaurant and the reception area both enjoy strong natural daylight, while the doors to the guest rooms look down onto the interior patio. A wrought iron banister with a wooden handrail adds the final touch.

Casa Figueres

1902
Antoni Ros Güell 1878-1954

Rambla, 83/Petxina, 1

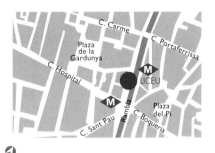

One of the sectors of society most enthusiastic about Modernism were the shopkeepers who hoped to attract more tasteful bourgeois clients–at the time strongly growing in numbers and purchasing power–by giving their shops a dash of distinction.

The shop, located on the ground floor of a building built in the nineteenth century, was founded in 1820 and remodelled by Antoni Ros in 1902. Ros was a remarkable landscape painter and scenographer. For him interior decoration was something he did occasionally but this did not prevent him from setting high standards.

For the Antigua Casa Figueras project Ros was backed up an excellent group of local artists and artisans. Collaborating together, they created a work of art in the heart of the city. The symbolic forms of the sculptures, the enamelled tessera mosaics, the stained glass and the classic Modernist typography of the old-style-advertising are all worthy of attention.

Today the shop, called Escribà, sells bread and cakes and is one of the most famous bakeries in Barcelona. Frequently the owners take advantage of the Modernist architectural backdrop to design "Modernist" cakes which recall the distinctive features and style of lettering of this movement.

The Casa Figueras is a splendid example of the lengths to which the artisans then went in their innovation. Their dedication can be appreciated in the mosaics, stained glass and the wrought iron of the two symmetrical façades. On the corner where they meet there is a depiction of the wheat harvest.

The Escribà cake shop has taken the art of confectionary and pastry making so far that it has become the cake shop par excellence in Barcelona. The outstanding Modernist look of the premises–in these photos we can see the tiled façade and the stained glass shop windows–has contributed decisively to this status.

Stained glass windows, a common recourse in Modernist design, transform the sunlight into multi-colored light inside the shop.

Reial Acadèmia de Ciències i Arts 1883

Josep Domènech i Estapà 1858-1917

Rambla, 115

The highlights of the Reial Acadèmia de Ciències i Arts are the staircase and vestibule, elegantly designed by the architect Josep Domènech i Estapà. However, what gives the building its personality is the clock on the façade because it used to mark official time in Barcelona.

Towards the end of the nineteenth century an official and accurate time-keeper was becoming necessary. Everybody relied on the clock they most trusted, the cathedral clock, the station clock, or whichever. In 1883 the City Hall decided to put an end to this confusing situation and created the municipal time-keeping service. A year later it was agreed that an astronomy observatory would be built in one of the two towers of the Reial Acadèmia. Despite different technical problems, and the budget, the time-keeping service of the Reial Acadèmia de Ciències i Arts was inaugurated in 1886. It would be responsible for keeping correct time for all the city.

This building's close relationship with clocks was intensified in 1985 when the Catalan poet Joan Brossa installed a visual poem in the vestibule of the Poliorama theatre, which today shares the building with the Academy. This visual poem is a fake clock facing away from the viewer in such a way that the observers see themselves reflected in the concave mirror which shows the time with clock hands going anti-clockwise.

Today the Reial Acadèmia de Ciències i Arts occupies the same building as the Poliorama theater. Add this to the fact that it is located on the Rambla, the city's busiest street, and you can understand why it is so frequently visited by the people of Barcelona.

In 1891 the Mayor decreed that this clock marked official Barcelona time, even though it was permitted a margin of error of one minute, reduced to one second when going by the pendulum clock in the institution's library.

The rooms of the Reial Acadèmia de Ciències i Arts are decorated with ornaments typical of Modernist art.

The façade of the old headquarters of the Editorial Montaner i Simon, crowned by the aluminium sculpture *Núvol i Cadira* (Cloud and Chair), brings together two innovative visions of art, one belonging to the building's creator, Lluís Domènech i Montaner, and the other belonging to the author of the emblematic sculpture, Antoni Tàpies. Today the latter's foundation is based in the building.

Editorial Montaner i Simon 1885

Lluís Domènech i Montaner 1850-1923

Carrer Aragó, 255

T his building was constructed between 1880 and 1885, sponsored by the maecenas Ramon Montaner, one of the architect's cousins who had amassed a great fortune with his publishing business and also financed other works by Domènech i Montaner. Even as early as 1880, the characteristic lines and style of Domènech's groundbreaking conception of architecture can be seen on this building, the first he designed in Barcelona. Later on he was to apply the same approach to his other emblematic constructions such as the Hospital de Sant Pau .

Together with Gaudí's Casa Vicens, this building is considered to be one of the key constructions of the beginning of the Modernist movement. However, it does not exploit the natural forms that were to become a classic part of this tendency. In contrast, there are marked Gothic style overtones and a discernible Mudejar influence. The façade reflects the architect's modern leanings, in the context of his times, as evidenced by the progressist symbols and the serrated lines a.

The building was designed for industrial useand therefore Domènech left the inside open-plan to take advantage of the daylight streaming in from the skylights overhead. Brick and iron were the materials he opted for, although up to that time they had usually been reserved for markets and train stations.

What before were the head offices of the publishing company Montaner i Simon have, since 1984, been the headquarters of the Fundació Antoni Tàpies which promotes the study and diffusion of Modern art. Inside the building there is a museum dedicated to this Catalan artist and a library specialising in Modern art and Asian art and culture. In 1987 the edifice was restored by the architects Roser Amadó and Lluís Domènech Girbau.

Casa Fargas 1904

Enric Sagnier 1858-1931

Rambla Catalunya, 47

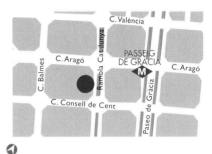

The Casa Fargas, located on Rambla Catalunya oppo-site the equally Modernist Casa Dolors Calm, is a clear example of how the movement delighted in gentle sweeping waves. The symmetrical façade, with the door pushed to one side, has a curved central tribune on all floors. It appears as if it were stuck on to the flat building. The arch around the door curves outwards and creatively distorts the growth of the surrounding vegetation. On both sides of the tribune the balcony rails imitate the wavy form of the centre of the building.

Sagnier decided to impose his own style in the vestibule. The lintels and rails are adorned with patterns which suggest vegetation in relief, and there are two trilobate arches dividing the space in two: on one side the elevator and on the other the staircase. The walls are decorated with sgraffito and the ochre marble skirting board is creatively cut out at the top. The fresco on the ceiling, the woodwork and the handrail–all of them conserved with reverence–deserve a mention in their own right.

This house, which belonged to the Dr. Miquel A. Fargas, is connected at the rear with his surgery where he used to receive his patients. The address was Carrer Consell de Cent 333, round the corner. A plaque bears testimony to the fact that here the politician and economist Ramon Trias i Fargas was born, lived and died (in 1989). Today the first floor is the headquarters of his eponymous foundation.

To design the Casa Fargas, Sagnier sidelined the gothic influence typical of his early work and went for a Modernista rococo style.

Inside, the house is a genuine work of art: walls, floors, pillars and banisters are enlivened with floral motifs. The surprisingly rich variety of ceiling lamps catches the eye.

The lamppost-benches designed by Pere Falqués, together with buildings like Antoni Gaudí's Casa Milà (the Pedrera), are one of the hallmarks of Passeig de Gràcia.

Lamppost-benches by Pere Falqués 1906

Pere Falqués 1850-1916

Passeig de Gràcia

Many residents of Barcelona wrongly think that it was the high-profile Modernist architect Antoni Gaudí who designed these playful creations along Barcelona's most important shopping street. It is a mistake difficult to get out of people's minds because their shapes are reminiscent of the Gaudinian forms of the Casa Batlló and Casa Milà on the same street. However, in fact the error serves to illustrate to what extent Falqués' design blends in harmoniously with the surrounding architectural context.

The lampposts-cum-benches consist of softly curved stone covered by a white ceramic mosaic pattern to form a bench in the shape of two back-to-back "L"s, perfect for sitting on and not just works of art. The wrought iron metallic structure which holds the lamp was welded into the bench by the local smithy Manuel Ballarín. The iron depicts floral patterns and the city's coat of arms.

This striking urban street furniture successfully combines the traditional street lamps of the nineteenth century with Modernist wrought-iron designs and mosaics. The commission with which Pere Falqués was charged was to contribute to the uniqueness of this boulevard, the home of the bourgeoisie in that period. Passeig de Gràcia was in those times–and still is–one of the principal thoroughfares of the city, connecting it to the old village of Gràcia (today one of the prettiest quarters of Barcelona).

After being neglected for many years these lampposts-cum-benches were restored to their former glory in the nineteen eighties.

The delicate elegance of this Modernist design is even more striking when compared with the backdrop of the heavy traffic along Barcelona's most famous boulevard.

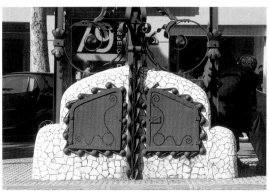

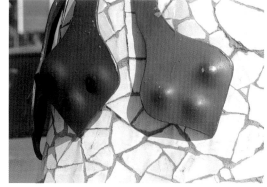

The project was commissioned to the specialist who frequently worked for the City Hall, Antoni de Falguera, who drew on the neogothic constructions of Josep Puig i Cadafalch such as the Casa Serra or the Casa Terrades, popularly referred to as the Casa de les Punxes.

Conservatori Municipal de Música 1916

Antoni de Falguera 1876-1945

Carrer Bruc, 112

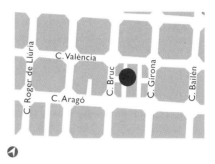

In this building, constructed when the Modernist movement was beginning to wane, hundreds of young musicians from all over Catalonia are trained.

The shape of the towers Antoni de Falguera designed reveal an identical approach to that used by Pere Falqués in the nearby municipal building in the Carrer Aragó. It is possible that Falqués was the author of the original project of the conservatory, which was then modified by Falguera in 1916.

Two twin towers unify the three exterior facades, emphasizing the central façade which stands higher than the lateral sides. On the two lateral fronts the ashlar stone cut has been used. The main door, framed by an Eusebi Arnau sculpture, is flanked by two small windows similar to those found on the third floor.

Inside, the most arresting elements are the staircase and the so called "peixera" (fishbowl) room, illuminated by a multi-coloured window overhead.

Antoni de Falguera designed this building so as to take as much advantage as possible of the natural light.

Music played by the pupils of the conservatory is the perfect complement to the building's Modernist charm. The ceilings, glasswork in the intrados, columns and floorings all stand out due to the care taken with the finishes.

A large window with stained glass framed by a lowered arch allowed for the floors below where work took place to be well illuminated. The balcony with the stone railing and floral decorations on the upper floor defined the private space belonging to its owner.

Casa Thomas 1898

Lluís Domènech i Montaner/Francesc Guàrdia Vial

Carrer Mallorca, 293

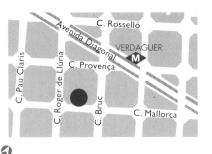

The Casa Thomas is an example of how one architect continuing on from the work of another can achieve a harmonious result. Lluís Domènech i Montaner was responsible for the early work of this building, with its neogothic façade. For the first time the architect introduced decorative elements which would later be standard in his works.

In its first version the building consisted of a semi-basement level, a first floor and a second floor. The two lower floors were given over to a workshop while the upper floor was for the owner's living quarters. The façade is a good reflection of the different uses of the building. A large window framed by an arch allowed plentiful light into the studio. The stone-balcony, complete with its floral patterns, marks off the more private area upstairs where the owner rested.

In 1912 his son-in-law, Francesc Guàrdia Vial, continued the project, obtaining Domènech's agreement to add on three more floors faithful to the original style of the project. The towers, reconstructed on the upper floor, and the original tile covering on all the façade are good examples of this continuity.

In 1979 a furniture shop opened on the ground floor. Its modern design contrasts with the original style. Domènech always defended vigorously the look he had given the building and the cohesion of the diverse styles.

The aesthetics of Modernism are found in all types of little details, right through from a brass handrail and stone columns to tiled coverings and squared glass panes.

A sculpture ensemble by Eusebi Arnau was also included. He engraved the image of a saw ("serra" in Catalan) on the medallions and coats of arms in honor of the family name.

Can Serra 1906

Josep Puig i Cadafalch 1869-1956

Rambla Catalunya, 126

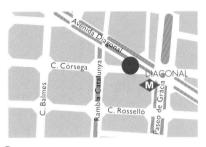

There is a curious story behind Can Serra. Started in 1900 when the architect and future President of the Diputació de Barcelona Josep Puig i Cadafalch was commissioned by the Serra family to build a palacete for one family on the elegant Rambla de Catalunya. Cadafalch designed a building which included elements of the Catalan Renaixança. Catalanism was just beginning to make itself felt and this was going to be expressed in the city's architecture.

Due to economics problems the family never moved in and in 1908 the building was sold to the Congregation of Santa Teresa de Jesús; they adapted it so that it could be used for teaching. Can Serra remained a college until 1969 when there came a period of uncertainty as to its future, speculation going as far as to consider its demolition. However, public opinion could not accept this idea and in 1985 the building was bought by the Diputació de Barcelona, of which Puig i Cadalfach had been President.

In 1987, a new building with a very modern look was opened on the rear façade of Can Serra. Its black tinted windows stand out among the features that contrast with the original style of Cadalfach. Some sectors of Barcelonian society felt that the work of the second team of architects that designed the redevelopment was not compatible with the medieval and historic idioms of the original creator, Puig i Cadalfach.

Casa Comalat 1911

Salvador Valeri 1873-1954

Avinguda Diagonal, 442

Although the official address of Casa Comalat is 442 Avinguda Diagonal, the widest avenue running all across Barcelona, the most impacting façade of this building designed by the architect Salvador Valeri, paradoxically the rear part, faces on to the Carrer Còrsega. It boasts a spectacular composition of colours, undeniably inspired by the Casa Batlló, work of the Modernist master Gaudí. The pastel tones dominate among the tiled mosaics and stained glass. The Modernist wooden galleries with their blinds sit comfortably beside the carpentry work and the polychrome ceramic edges. The crowning pediment, covered by a mosaic, finishes off the Gaudinian touch on the façade.

Yet maybe the most interesting part of this building lies inside. The extraordinarily beautiful vestibule is furnished with rounded benches, lamps and mosaics.

Unfortunatly, during the building's restoration in 1987 some sculptures of female figures which flanked the dome of the main façade were damaged and had to be got rid off.

The main façade, on Avinguda Diagonal is much more low-key even though it too does adopt the curved lines so typical of Gaudí. However, the final look is completely different. An example of the restrained style of this side of the building are the two sets of medieval horse-armour found in the entrance. The tribune balcony stands out from the rest of the façade, crowned by a dome covered by glazed green tiles.

Palau del Baró de Quadras 1904

Josep Puig i Cadafalch 1869-1956

Avinguda Diagonal, 373

The Palau del Baró de Quadras is the result of an exhaustive reform of a private home carried out by Josep Puig i Cadafalch. The building, located on a particularly narrow block, clearly reveals the artist's intentions with each of the different façades. The façades, one on Carrer Rosselló and the other on Avinguda Diagonal suggest two completely different design approaches.

The main façade faces out over Diagonal and has the classic look of the houses, or the little palaces in which just one family live, of the nobility in the Gothic epoch. Under the tribune balcony there is a sculpture ensemble by Eusebi Arnau. One of the sculptures is of Saint Jordi, the patron saint of Catalonia, slaying the dragon.

Around the corner, in the Carrer Rossellón 279, is the other façade. Any uninformed observer would be unable to guess that the two designs were part of the same building. The building is typical of the Eixample area of Barcelona, and is one of many inhabited by various families with their own flat. The patio staircase and the sgraffito work in the wall vaults are the most noteworthy features.

Today the Palau del Baró de Quadras houses the Museo de la Música. A trip round its complete set of instruments explains how music has evolved since the sixteenth century. The pianos belonging to the musicians Joaquim Malats, Amadeu Vives and Otto Kibuntz, and the six organs, one of which dates back to the eighteenth century where it was installed in the now-disappeared Santa Caterina convent, are particularly fascinating.

The staircase is probably the feature which draws the most gasps in this patio, an area which Cadalfach always gave great importance to. In this particular case he focused his efforts on the spectacular stonework of the banister and the grey tones of wavy-patterned floor ceramics. Neither did he hold back on the attention he dedicated to the lower part of the walls.

Casa Macaya 1903

Josep Puig i Cadafalch 1869-1956

Passeig Sant Joan, 108

Shortly after completing the Casa Amatller, one of his most famous works, Puig i Cadafalch started work on another architectural jewel of his so-called pink period –in honour of the colour of the bricks. The Casa Macaya is an original construction which combines gothic style influences, so attractive to the Modernist architects, with clearly Mudejar touches.

The building project was based on the idea of a home for one family. Puig wanted to emphasize the ornamentation of the stone window frames of the façade by contrasting it against the white stucco sgraffitos. Two late-gothic doors, similar to those on the Casa Amatller, stand out. They are adorned by an ensemble of sculptures by Eusebi Arnau depicting everyday scenes like a farmer on a donkey or the architect himself riding a bike, his normal means of transport to get around the city, something which Arnau wanted to immortalize in one of his emblematic constructions.

The interior is in no way inferior to the external aspect but today little remains that indicates that it was once a residence. The original tiles and sgraffitos remain in the vestibule, and the patio, with its open staircase typical of the city's Medieval palaces, is still intact.

Today the Casa Macaya belong to the Caixa d'Estalvis i Pensions de Barcelona" (a savings bank) and is the headquarters of its foundation. Numerous art expositions are held in the building and there is a well-equipped library and resource centre.

The Casa Macaya is an example of a privately owned Modernist building heavily visited by the public. Numerous art expositions are put on here.

The rooms inside have little left of their original look. The different uses given to them over the years have completely changed their aspect.

Museu de Zoologia

1888

Lluís Domènech i Montaner 1850-1923

Parc de la Ciutadella

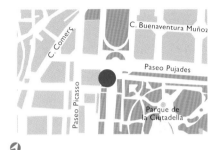

The story of the building which today houses the city's zoological museum is one of abrupt changes in destiny. The building, situated within the Parc de la Ciutadella and designed by Lluís Doménech i Montaner, was originally intended to be the grand café-restaurant of the Exposiciò Universal in Barcelona in 1888. However, the café was never finished.

Once the exposition was over the architect set up a workshop there for artisans to work on decorative arts. Shortly afterwards a history museum was housed there and from 1896 through to 1902 the building was the home of the Escola Municipal de Música, today in the Carrer Bruc. In 1917 the Museu de Catalunya, dedicated to the flowers, fauna and geology of Catalonia, moved in. During the years of the Republic the building was used as a job centre, a school registration office and even as a dining room for the hard up. Before it ended up as the Museu de Zoologia is was a museum of biology.

The building is commonly referred to as El Castell dels Tres Dragons ("The Castle of the Three Dragons"). Domènech i Montaner drew his inspiration from the Catalan Gothic and Mudejar architecture, adding in a German touch. The result is a medieval looking building, the contrast of the bricks bringing out the power of expression of the iron. The four towers and the large heraldic shields give the building its medieval mark.

The city's zoological museum is located in one of Barcelona's best-loved parks. The zoo and the Parlament de Catalunya are also there.

The Modernist Route. Continuation

See *Barcelona. Gaudí and Modernism (First volume)*

16. Palau Güell 1886

Carrer Nou de la Rambla, 3-5

17. Mercat de la Boqueria 1874

Rambla, 91

18. Els 4 Gats 1894

Carrer Montsió, 3

19. Palau de la Música Catalana 1905

Carrer Sant Pere Més Alt, 13

20. Casa Calvet 1900

Carrer Casp, 48

21. Casa Lleó Morera 1902

Passeig de Gràcia, 35

22. Casa Amatller 1898

Passeig de Gràcia, 41

25. Casa Milà, la Pedrera 1906

Passeig de Gràcia, 92

23. Casa Batlló 1905

Passeig de Gràcia, 43

24. Palau Montaner 1889

Carrer Mallorca, 278

28. Hospital de Sant Pau 1905

Carrer Sant Antoni Maria Claret, 169

26. Casa Terrades 1903

Avinguda Diagonal, 416

27. Sagrada Família 1881

Plaça de la Sagrada Família

29. Parc Güell 1900

Carrer Olot, s/n

30. Casa Vicens 1883

Carrer Carolines, 18-24

31. Cafè de l'Òpera 1929

Rambla, 74

32. Casa Dr. Genové

Rambla, 77

33. Nadal pharmacy 1850

Rambla, 121

34. Ateneu Barcelonès 1836

Carrer Canuda, 6

36. Casa Pascual i Pons 1891

Passeig de Gràcia, 2-4

37. Forn Sarret

Carrer Girona, 73

35. Catalana de Gas 1895

Portal de l'Àngel, 20-22

38. Cases Rocamora 1917

Passeig de Gràcia, 6-14

39. Casa Dolors Calm 1902

Rambla Catalunya, 54

40. Bolós pharmacy 1902

Rambla Catalunya, 77

41. Casa Juncosa 1907

Rambla Catalunya, 76-78

42. C. Josep i Ramón Queraltó 1907

Rambla Catalunya, 88

43. Casa Josefa Villanueva 1909

Carrer València, 312

44. Casa Jaume Forn 1904

Carrer València, 285

45. Casa Llopis Bofill

Carrer Bailèn, 113

46. Casa Sayrach 1918

Avinguda Diagonal, 423

47. Casa Bonaventura Ferrer 1906

Passeig de Gràcia, 113

48. Casa Fuster

Passeig de Gràcia, 132

49. Casa Planells 1924

Avinguda Diagonal, 332

* The museum includes a rich collection of Catalan art from the middle of the 19th century to the 1930s.

50. Museu d'Art Modern *

Parc de la Ciutadella

1. Plaça Reial lampposts
2. Hotel España
3. Hotel Peninsular
4. Casa Figueres
5. Reial Acadèmia de Ciències i Arts
6. Editorial Montaner i Simon
7. Casa Fargas
8. Lampoost-benches by Pere Falqués
9. Conservatori Municipal de Música
10. Casa Thomas
11. Can Serra
12. Casa Comalat
13. Palau del Baró de Quadras
14. Casa Macaya
15. Museu de Zoologia
16. Palau Güell
17. Mercat de la Boqueria
18. Els 4 Gats
19. Palau de la Música
20. Casa Calvet
21. Casa Lleó Morera
22. Casa Amatller
23. Casa Batlló
24. Palau Montaner
25. Casa Milà, la Pedrera

26. Casa Terrades, Casa de les Punxe
27. Temple de la Sagra Família
28. Hospital de la Sant Creu i Sant Pau
29. Parc Güell, Casa Museu Gaudi
30. Casa Vicens
31. Cafè de l'Òpera
32. Casa Dr. Genové
33. Nadal pharmacy
34. Ateneu Barcelonès
35. Catalana de Gas
36. Casa Pascual i Po
37. Forn Sarret
38. Cases Rocamora
39. Casa Dolors Calm
40. Bolós pharmacy
41. Casa Juncosa
42. Casa Josep i Ram Queraltó
43. Casa Josefa Villan
44. Casa Jaume Forn
45. Casa Llopis i Bofil
46. Casa Sayrach
47. Casa Bonaventura Ferrer
48. Casa Fuster
49. Casa Planells
50. Museu d'Art Mode

Glossary

Chaflán The staggered corners formed when two streets cross; very common in the centre of Barcelona after the urban redevelopment carried out according to Ildefons Cerdà's plan in 1859.

Eixample The name given to the city centre area of Barcelona after Ildefons Cerdà's urban project had been executed.

Frieze Any decorative band on an outer wall bearing lettering or sculpture in low relief.

Glazed tessellate Small squares or blocks of tiles arranged in a chequered or mosaic pattern for floors or pavements.

Gothic style Art developed and evolving out of Romanic art in western Europe from the twelfth century through to the Renaissance.

Heraldic shield Sculptures which depict symbols representing the ancestry of noble families.

Intrados The interior curve or surface of an arch or vault.

Lamppost-bench Unique L-shaped benches which also act as the base out of which rises up a lamppost. They are found on Passeig de Gràcia.

Mosaic A decoration consisting of tiny pieces of inlaid stone or glass.

Medallion A tablet, often circular, which bears objects represented in relief.

Mudejar art Art created in Spain under Moorish influence from the thirteenth century through to the sixteenth. It is characterized by the fusion of elements of Christian art and Arab ornamentation.

Pediment Triangular gable-end area, often filled with sculpture.

Portico A structure made up of a roof supported by columns. A porticoed square has this type of porch running around its sides.

Sgraffito Ornamentation in which the top layer of paint, plaster or clay solution is incised to reveal the contrasting colour of the ground.

Tessera Each of the small pieces used in mosaic work.

Trencadís A Catalan word which refers to the decorative patterns created by Antoni Gaudí by recycling little ceramic pieces or shards.

Trilobed arch An arch, the intrados of which have three lobes.

Practical information

ℹ Centre del Modernisme

Passeig de Gràcia, 43 (Casa Amatller)

Tel.: 934 880 139

www.rutamodernisme.com

Opening times: Monday to Saturday. 10 a.m. to 7 p.m. Sundays and Holidays, 10 a.m. to 2 p.m.

The center offers a pass which enables the holder to obtain a discount of up to 50% on the entrance fee to all the buildings on the tour. It is valid for one month. Six times a day, in English and Spanish, there is a talk in the center about de façades of the Modernist buildings on the "block of dissension" (so called bacause of the different styles). The buildings in question, not open to the public, are Casa Batlló, Casa Amatller and Casa Lleó Morera. A schedule is available for consulation.

You can visit other web sites to find out more about Modernism:

www.gaudiclub.com

www.barcelona-on-line.es

www.horitzo.es/expo2000.

Tours

The visits to buildings listed bellow all start out from the same point, plaça Catalunya.

1. Plaça Reial lamp standards

Plaça Reial

Metro LICEU (line 3)

Go down la Rambla from Plaça Catalunya until you come to Carrer Colom, on the left. It leads into the square.

2. Hotel España

Carrer Sant Pau, 9-11

The restaurant can be visited when meals are not being served

Free entrance

Metro LICEU (line 3)

The hotel is very near to the corner of the Rambla and the Carrer Sant Pau.

3. Hotel Peninsular

Carrer Sant Pau, 34

The inside can be visited but only in the mornings

Free entrance

Metro LICEU (line 3)

Go down the Rambla and take the Carrer Sant Pau to the right.

4. Casa Figueres

Rambla, 83/Petxina, 1

Opening times: 8,30 a.m. to 9 p.m. daily

Metro LICEU (line 3)

As you go down la Rambla you will find it just after going past the market.

5. Reial Acadèmia de Ciències i Arts

Rambla, 115

Not open to the public

Metro CATALUNYA (lines 1 and 3)

Go down la Rambla towards the sea using the pavement on the right. The Acadèmia is after the second street on the right.

6. Editorial Montaner i Simon

Carrer Aragó, 255

Opening times: Tuesday to Sunday, 10 a.m. to 8 p.m.

Metro PASSEIG DE GRÀCIA (lines 2, 3 and 4)

Go up Rambla Catalunya from Plaça Catalunya until you come to Carrer Aragó. The building is on the other side of the street, very near the corner.

7. Casa Fargas

Rambla Catalunya, 47

Not open to the public

Metro PASSEIG DE GRÀCIA (lines 2, 3 and 4)

Go up Rambla Catalunya. The house is two blocks after Gran Via de les Corts Catalanes.

8. Lampposts-beches by Pere Falqués

Passeig de Gràcia

Bus line 24. Metro PASSEIG DE GRÀCIA (lines 2, 3 and 4)

These lampposts are all along both sides of this boulevard.

9. Conservatori Municipal de Música

Carrer Bruc, 112

Opening times: 9 a.m. to 9 p.m. except Sunday and Holiday

Free entrance

Metro GIRONA (line 4)

Go up Passeig de Gràcia, turn right on the Carrer València and go along it until you come to the Carrer Bruc.

10. Casa Thomas

Carrer Mallorca, 293

Not open to the public

Metro DIAGONAL (line 3)

Go up the right hand side of Passeig de Gràcia until you come to the Carrer Mallorca. Go along Mallorca for two blocks and you will arrive at the house.

11. Can Serra

Rambla Catalunya, 126

Not open to the public

Metro DIAGONAL (lines 3 y 5), VERDAGUER (line 4)

Go up Rambla Catalunya until you come to the Carrer Rosselló. The building is on the corner with Avinguda Diagonal.

12. Casa Comalat

Avinguda Diagonal, 442

Not open to the public

Metro VERDAGUER (line 4)

Take metro line 4 at the station in Gran Via/Passeig de Gràcia. You do not have to change trains. When you come out of VERDAGUER station, cross over the avenue to get to the building.

13. Palau del Baró de Quadras

Avinguda Diagonal, 373

Opening times: Tuesday, Thursday, riday Saturday and Sunday, 10 a.m. to 2 p.m.; Wednesday, 10 a.m. to 8 p.m.

Entrance must be paid

Metro DIAGONAL (lines 3 and 5)

Pick up metro line 3 in Plaça Catalunya. Get off at DIAGONAL station, the second stop. Once you are up in the street (Passeig de Gràcia), go along Carrer Rosselló until you come to the corner with Avinguda Diagonal.

14. Casa Macaya

Passeig Sant Joan, 108

Opening time: 11 a.m. to 20 p.m.

Free entrance

Metro VERDAGUER (lines 4 and 5)

Take metro line 4 at PASSEIG DE GRÀCIA station. Get off at VERDAGUER station. The building is right by the subway entrance.

15. Museu de Zoologia

Parc de la Ciutadella

Opening times: Tuesday, Wednesday, Friday, Saturday and Sunday, from 10 a.m. to 2 p.m; Thursday, from 10 a.m. to 6.30 p.m.; Monday closed.

Entrance must be paid

Metro ARC DE TRIOMF (line 1)

Take metro line 1 from Plaça Catalunya. Once outside, go along Passeig Lluís Companys until you come to the park. The museum is to the right on the edge of the park.

Other titles by Kliczkowski Publishers

Fundición, 15 Polígono Industrial Santa Ana 28529 Rivas-Vaciamadrid Madrid Tel. 34 91 666 50 01 Fax 34 91 301 26 83 asppan@asppan.com www.onlybook.com

78

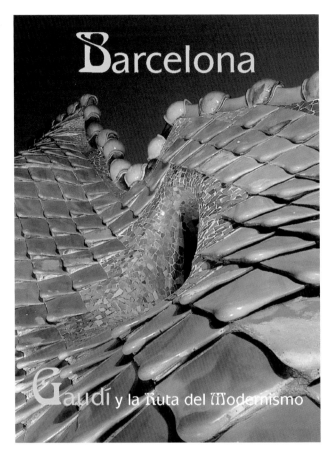

Barcelona, Gaudí y la Ruta del Modernismo/Barcelona, Gaudí and Modernism

ISBN (E): 84-89439-50-4 Spanish text

ISBN (GB): 84-89439-51-1 English text

ISBN (D): 84-89439-58-3 German text

ISBN (IT): 84-89439-59-1 Italian text

The Best of Lofts
ISBN (E/GB): 95-09575-84-4

The Best of Bars & Restaurants
ISBN (E/GB): 95-09575-86-8

The Best of American Houses
ISBN (E/GB): 98-79778-17-0

Interiores minimalistas/Minimalist Interiors
ISBN (E/GB): 98-79778-16-6

Lofts minimalistas/Minimalist lofts
ISBN (E/GB): 84-89439-55-9

Estancias Argentinas
ISBN (E/GB): 98-79778-19-7

Guggenheim
ISBN (E): 84-89439-52-4
ISBN (GB): 84-89439-53-5
ISBN (D): 84-89439-54-2

Los encantos de Barcelona/
Barcelona Style
ISBN (E): 84-89439-56-7
ISBN (GB): 84-89439-57-5

Hotels. Designer & Design
Hoteles. Arquitectura y Diseño
ISBN (E/GB): 84-89439-61-3

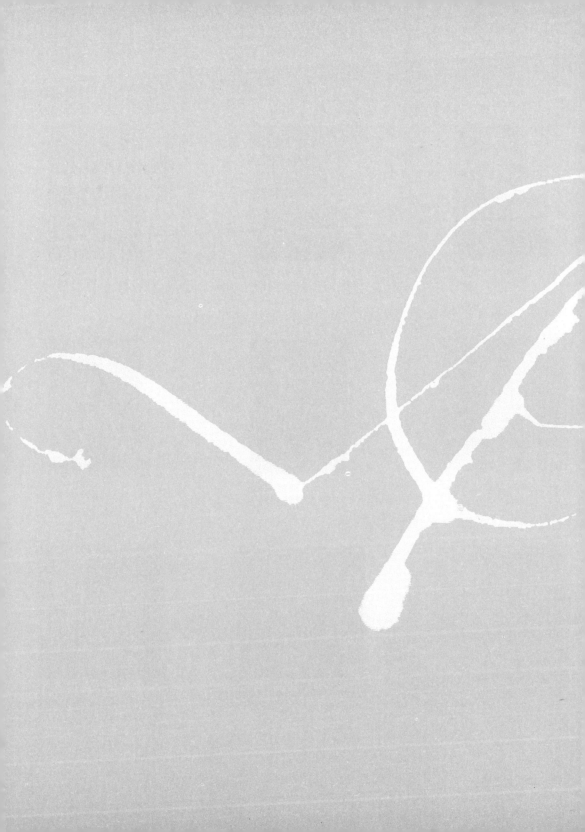